Timeless Reflections

For Everyday Living

A 30 Day Devotional

JOYCE KIRIMI

Timeless Devotions for Everyday Living: A 30 Day Devotional

Copyright © 2020 Joyce Kirimi
ISBN: 978-9966-69-041-8

Published by

PUBLISHING
Institute of Africa

P.O. Box 16458 – 00100
NAIROBI
KENYA

info@publishing-institute.org
www.publishing-institute.org

CONTENTS

DEDICATION

I dedicate this book to my mother, Faith Nyambura, who made a priceless effort to introduce me to church and laid the strong Christian foundation in my life.

ACKNOWLEDGEMENT

I am grateful to God, who rescued my life from the pit, secured me for Himself and continues to teach me how to know him more each day.

I am grateful to my loving husband Kirimi, and my best friend, Sue, who encourage me to write and always give me unwavering support.

I acknowledge my family and friends who have unreservedly shared their lives with me and whose life experiences have provided and continue to offer precious life lessons for me when I reflect.

I am indebted to my publisher and all the professionals who worked hard to transform my reflective thoughts into a book.

I have always known Joyce as a passionate worship leader and therefore expected that the first book she might write, would have nothing but anything to do with worship. However, through *Timeless Reflections for Everyday Living*, I now realise where she draws the spirit of worship from. You cannot worship the God whom you have not devoted yourself to spend time in His presence. Meaningful worship emanates from a rich devotion. To all ministers of God, regardless of your calling, Joyce is inviting us to her devotional life and learn the source of every authentic ministry acceptable to our God.

First, *Timeless Reflections for Everyday Living*, has not been born from the desire to write a book or another devotional book; rather, the desire is based on her sharing her practical devotional experience with God. The book is an honest and practical narrative of a real devotional encounter with God. Joyce has chosen to share her "eureka" moments with the Word of God. It is her personal experience without any human intervention. To use Paul's own words when he wrote to the Galatians in defence of the gospel he preached: *"I did not receive it from any man, nor was I taught it; rather, I received it by revelation from Jesus Christ."* (1:12; NIV). *Timeless Reflections for Everyday Living* has proved that everyone is capable of their "eureka" moment, and Joyce is benevolent enough to invite us to cultivate the same lifestyle of devotion.

Secondly, the reflective questions at the end of every chapter further invite the reader into a personal search for personal spirituality leading to spiritual growth which is grounded on the personal encounter of God through a personal devotion. Meaningful Spiritual growth is based on that solitary moment when it is just you and God; that wrestling with God, that *"I will not let you go unless you bless me"* (Gen. 32:24-26).

Thirdly, the reflective questions are also useful for group discussions and devotions; that is for two or more people seeking the Lord together in sharing their experiences and personal stories. In each study, the reader is invited to connect with the day to day challenges he or she might be facing.

Fourthly, the book will help the reader in connecting or relating real-life situations with scripture. The Bible, instead of addressing only the audience of thousands of years ago, through application to contextual issues, Joyce has made the Bible "alive" and easy to relate with. People find themselves asking, how can the Bible be an answer to the complex and painful experiences they are going through today?

Finally, this is a precious gift to the body of Christ, and especially for those who have been struggling with personal devotions. You now have a tool from which you can draw some lessons to carry out your devotions. I welcome you to join Joyce in a worship devotion. Knowing Joyce as a passionate worship leader and a worshipper of God, definitely in this devotion, there is a taste of worship.

It is, therefore, my humble pleasure and a great honour to write a foreword and to recommend *Timeless Reflections for Everyday Living* for the spiritual transformation of God's people, not only to live victoriously here on earth but above all, to be prepared for everlasting communion with God.

Rev. Dr. Simon J. Oriedo

Curate & Director of Missions and Evangelism Pillar
ACK St. Mark's Church Westlands - Nairobi Diocese

As we walk through life, we all encounter different situations at different seasons. At the end of each encounter, we often look back and try to figure out what it was all about or even try to let our experience with that encounter just sink in. As we do this, we may discover that the encounter brought some lessons our way while other times, we just let the experience pass and we don't draw any lesson. At times we may even draw lessons from the experiences of other people. Upon reflections, we may discover that some experiences bring us closer to God by focusing more on him and loving Him more while others draw us further from Him. Some experiences may even influence our relationships with other people.

No matter what experiences we encounter in our lives, the essential thing is that we reflect on them and allow those encounters to change our lives positively. The most fundamental positive change that can happen in our lives is relating to God better and more intimately.

Timeless Reflections for Everyday Living is a collection of reflections on God's unconditional love and our relationship and service to him while we are alive. The reflections are drawn from my own experiences, experiences of others and also experiences of characters drawn from scripture. They help us look at our lives in connection with our relationship with God in many aspects.

At the end of each reflection, there are some reflective questions to help us look reflectively inward and take time to connect with ourselves more as we grow our intimacy with God.

May you find each reflection refreshing and enriching. May the reflections challenge you to always reflect upon your life experiences and may you draw positive lessons from each encounter in consonance with God's word and purpose for your life.

GOD'S LOVE
AND
HERITAGE

GOD IS MINDFUL OF YOU

It is so amazing to consider God, thinking how big he is, how awesome, how magnificent and, how majestic he is. God is indeed indescribable through human terms. No words could describe his divine nature. No space or house can contain him. Heaven is his throne and the earth is his footstool (Isaiah 66:1). God's ways and thoughts are so much higher than our ways and thoughts and hence it is difficult to comprehend him in our simple human minds (Isaiah 55:8-9).

When I consider this great God of creation, and the work of his hands, it's amazing and truly humbling. It is no wonder that scientists have spent entire lifetimes trying to unravel the wonder in God's creation. They are still trying. Science has not yet succeeded in explaining the wonders of nature around us. Yet, all these wonders depict the powerful God. They express the magnificence of his handiwork. From the heavens above to the sea below, it

When I consider your heavens, the work of your fingers, the moon and the stars, which you have set in place, what is mankind that you are mindful of them, human beings that you care for them?

(NIV)

all reflects his glory. And yet, as big as God is and as great as his works are, he is mindful of humans and he cares for us as the psalmist says in Psalm 8:3-4. In fact, our special place in God's heart spans back to creation. God made everything by his word and on the sixth day, when it came to the creation of humans, God chose to make us in His own image (Genesis 1:26-27).

Despite the fall, God was still so mindful of humans and cared for the restoration of the relationship with them that he made a way to reconcile us and gave his only begotten Son to be born as a man and later die on the cross to redeem and reconcile us. John 3:16 says, *"For God so loved the world that he gave his one and only son, that whoever believes in him shall not perish but have eternal life."(NIV)* What a lovely revelation of how important we are to the Maker of heaven and earth.

1 *Do you ever look down upon yourself or belittle yourself because of your background, identity, race, education, etc.?*

2 *Has anyone ever made you feel small or unimportant?*

3 *Do you realize how important you are to God and that he is mindful of every detail of your life?*

Lord, help me embrace the revelation and the reality of how wonderful you are and yet how mindful you are of me. Once I embrace it, help me learn to love you and honour you always. Amen.

God is mindful of you

MY GRACE IS SUFFICIENT

Paul had visions and revelations of paradise from the Lord as he commented in 2 Corinthians 12: 1-6. He said he desired to refrain from boasting except in his infirmities so that no one would think of him above what he saw him to be or what he heard him say.

But he also reveals in 12:7 that, to keep him from being exalted above measure by the abundance of those visions and revelations, he suffered a thorn in the flesh, a messenger of Satan to buffet him lest he be exalted above measure. In other words, the thorn served as a check against his exaltation, his pride, his elevation or boastfulness.

This thorn in the flesh may have been a physical or spiritual infirmity or trial or tribulation – the Bible does not clarify this. But whatever form it took, it definitely troubled Paul and he pleaded with God three times that it be removed. The Lord responded that his grace was sufficient for Paul and his strength is made perfect in weakness.

And he said to me, "My grace is sufficient for you, for my strength is made perfect in weakness." Therefore most gladly I will rather boast in my infirmities, that the power of Christ may rest upon me.

(NKJV)

This seems to mean that God allowed Paul to be in such a situation of insufficiency so that his grace could be seen as sufficient. When Paul was weak, God's strength could be perfected in his life.

At some moments in our lives we also may experience such great insufficiency and weakness that we constantly plead with God to remove these troubles and woes from our lives. The irony is that when our lives seem to be thriving on one end, there seems to be humbling trouble on the other. Just when you got that job you've always dreamt of, your teenage child becomes rebellious; just when your marriage is on a high, the doctors discover your inability to bear children; just when your career is thriving and in its peak, your parents fall ill and you have to take care of them.

The truth of the matter is that some of these 'thorns in the flesh' are here to stay in order to prevent pride and boastfulness. These are not going to be removed because they keep us from being exalted above measure. In our human nature, it is easy to boast and take pride in our achievements.

The greatest joy in these troubles is that we are constantly reminded that his grace is sufficient. As we recognize our weakness his strength is perfected in our lives. Whether our insufficiency and weakness is spiritual or physical, his strength is made perfect.

REFLECTIVE QUESTIONS

1   *What infirmities, reproaches, persecutions or tribulations are you facing today?*
2   *For whose sake do you face these troubles?*
3   *Do you seek that they be removed from you or do you seek God's grace to carry through?*

. . . .

Dear Lord, help me realize that some tribulations will not go away and teach me to take pleasure in my infirmities, reproaches, needs, persecution, distress, tribulations, or in troubles, for your sake so that when I am weak then I am strong in you. Amen.

. . . .

My grace is sufficient

GOD'S JUDGMENT IS NOT BIASED

When we consider the earthly justice system, it is easy to have a lot of questions left in our minds. It is easy to notice that some judgments given in the courts of law are biased or wrong or misplaced. One does not need to be a legal expert to decipher the errors in some of these judgments. At times, cases are decided with so much partiality that you might not want to seek justice in the judicial system for fear that instead of justice, you will receive injustice. In fact that is why many people are sorting out issues in their own style, ignoring law and formal justice systems.

It is not so with our God. The justice system of Jehovah God is entirely flawless and unbiased. No matter what or who faces his justice system, there is never any bias or partiality in his judgments.

Unlike our earthly judicial systems that are easily corrupted and manipulated depending on the social or economic status of the accused or the aggrieved person, God judges all impartially. Isaiah 24:2 makes it clear that the people are just like the priest, that the servant and the master are alike, that the maid and her mistress have no difference, the buyer and the seller are the same, as are the lender and the borrower, the creditor and the debtor. All face the same law. Status, power, wealth, knowledge, religiosity and the like have no effect on his judgment. God indeed shows no partiality nor takes a bribe (Deuteronomy 10:17; 2 Chronicles 19:7).

The Lord God is so just and impartial that we must be careful how we conduct ourselves because at judgment time we will have no room to manipulate him. He shall repay us according to what we have done (Job 34:11). We shall reap what we have sown because our God is not mocked (Galatians 6:7). Everybody shall receive what they deserve according to their deeds.

REFLECTIVE QUESTIONS

1. *Have you ever encountered an injustice in your life whether at family, office or government level?*
2. *How did it make you feel?*
3. *Have you ever felt that God is unfair or unjust on any matter concerning your life?*

....

Dear heavenly Father, I know you are a just God. Please help me walk rightly and sow appropriately so that at the time of reaping I will not be embarrassed as I receive my reward from you, because I know your judgment is just. Amen

....

God's judgment is not biased

CLOUD BY DAY, FIRE BY NIGHT

When it is so hot and the sun is scorching, we all wish for a cool shade, an air conditioned room or at least some sort of cover over our heads and bodies lest we suffer heat stroke. But then again, when the hours change and evening arrives, it not only becomes dark but it also becomes chilly. In winter, night time temperatures become extremely cold and almost unbearable. The darkness is equally deep and untenable.

How convenient it was for the Israelites during those days when the Lord's cloud covered them by day. They did not have to endure extreme heat. While it ought to have been hot and scorching, they enjoyed the coolness that the Lord provided. And when night time came, with the darkness and cold it brings, the Lord provided a fire in the cloud – to light their way and keep them warm. The Lord was all that they needed through their travels and they did not have to look far to find him because he was so present with them by day and by night. Who would have thought of the shade and cooling provided by a cloud by day and the lighting and warmth provided by fire at night? The Lord made it all happen for them.

It does not matter the kind of journey we are on today. The Lord is able to provide all we require for our life. When he is present in our journey, he knows exactly what we need and so we do not have to worry about anything. But if his presence is not with us, we are in trouble. No wonder Moses told God that they would not move if his presence did not go with them (Exodus 33:15). God will certainly provide the exact cover and shield that we need in every circumstance of our life's journey. If illumination is needed, he knows how, when, where and with what to light our way because he is a lamp unto our feet and a light unto our path (Psalm 119:105). If we need warmth, the Lord has his design and style of providing it regardless of where we are. He is not short of ideas. He is not ignorant or unaware of our situations (John 10:14). He knows and understands our journey. He knows our fears. He knows exactly what we need when we need it (Philippians 4:19). He shall provide whether by cloud or by fire.

1   *Do you at times feel alone and abandoned and even think that God is not there?*

2   *Have you ever felt very exposed to the ills and evils of this world?*

3   *Are you aware that if you have invited his presence into your life, God will never leave you alone whether by day or by night?*

. . . .

Lord, may you light my path daily and help me to always be aware of your presence in my life. Amen.

. . . .

Cloud by day, fire by night

MY BOUNDARY LINES

In Kenya, there is an obsession with land acquisition. People work very hard to make sure that they have a piece of land or property somewhere in their name. Some are able to buy it for themselves with their own money. There is also a great attachment to ancestral or inherited land. Those entitled to a portion in inheritance always hope that theirs will be in the best location but that is not always the case because while one heir will end up in the good location, everyone else must end up with a farther one. This may at times result in siblings fighting among themselves and even fighting it in the courts as they argue about borders and boundaries. Sometimes people feel that they have ended up with a good inheritance and that those distributing the inheritance or the surveyors involved somewhat favoured them. On the other hand, some people end up manipulating or corrupting their parents (especially if they are old or ailing) or the surveyors so that they can end up with boundary lines where they wanted or desired them to be.

We equally have our lot in the kingdom of God. In fact, God is our portion of inheritance and he is the one who maintains our lot. Though we do not have physical boundary lines in the heavenly kingdom, we have God himself as our inheritance (Ezekiel 44:28; Numbers 18:20).

We have come to the knowledge of Christ, not through our own doing but by his grace and are therefore co-heirs with Christ (Romans 8:17). Our inheritance is incorruptible and safely kept in heaven for us (1 Peter 1:4). We are rich and wealthy not in what brings forth misery or which rots and is eaten by moths; not the richness of gold and silver that corrodes with time (James 5:1-6). We instead boast in the riches we have found in knowing Christ (Ephesians 3:8; Colossians 1:27; 2:2) which is the greatest inheritance of all.

What a pleasant place our lines have fallen in. What a good inheritance we have in God himself, that while we were still sinners destined to eternal death, he by his mercies ransomed us and has given

us himself as an inheritance. We have life eternal by knowing him (John 17:3). What better inheritance could we get? Where else could we wish for our boundary lines to have fallen?

REFLECTIVE QUESTIONS

1. *From where do you get your daily portion?*
2. *Who or what secures your life? Is it your education, your job, your business, your bank balance or your property?*
3. *Have you determined your boundaries in Christ?*

Lord, help me recognize where the boundary lines have fallen for me and that the heritage I have in you is sufficient and my lot in you is secure. Amen.

MY HERITAGE

If you have ever been the victim of a weaponised attack or an armed robbery, then the mention of weapon may be familiar and even traumatizing. Depending on the nature and extent of the attack and how close or personal it was, the familiarity and trauma varies. Another issue is that of tongues rising against us. If you are an African, I imagine that while growing up, you experienced some sort of warning from your parent or guardian to be wary of some relative or neighbour lest they curse or bewitch you or cast a spell on you. When bad things happen to people in some families they are attributed to a relative or neighbour who either spoke against them or did something to cause this harm. Some of these are seen as purely traditional superstitions while others are actual works of the devil through human agency.

And while these evils may seem far-fetched or imaginary, especially when we have never encountered them, they are real. The Bible confirms that and thus we cannot wish them away (Genesis 12:3;

Exodus 21:17; Proverbs 20:20; Luke 6:28). Evil is present in our world, happens in our lives and is indeed present in our generation.

The victory in our hands is the promised heritage for the servants of the Lord. He has promised that no weapon forged or turned or aimed against us shall succeed. Here, we must deliberately shift our focus from the earthly, physical weapons to consider our tools for war. The weapons of our warfare are not carnal but divine, in order to demolish strongholds (2 Corinthians 10:4-5). We wrestle against principalities and powers, against rulers of darkness and spiritual hosts of wickedness. But the weapons formed against us and the tongues raised against us in the heavenly places by the hosts of wickedness shall not prevail. That is our heritage. Clearly, weapons will be formed against us, attacks will be targeted at us, war will be waged against us, tongues will be raised against us, and curses will be pronounced on us but we shall conquer them in Jesus' name.

Our Lord Jesus Christ already disarmed the principalities and powers and triumphed over them (Colossians 2:15) and because he is sovereign over all principalities and powers, we are complete in him (Colossians 2:10). We have a divine heritage of conquest in the heavenly realms through his righteousness in us.

REFLECTIVE QUESTIONS

1   *Are there any weapons the enemy has established against your life?*
2   *Are there tongues and voices that have been rising against you in contradiction to God's promises for your life?*
3   *How can you claim your heritage and righteousness in God for your divine destiny?*

Dear God, help me recognize and acknowledge my heritage in you and henceforth live a life of righteousness in you. Amen.

SALVATION, RENEWAL & RESTORATION

RESTORED, STRONG, FIRM, AND STEADFAST

Jesus said that in this world we will have many troubles but we can take heart because he has overcome the world. This prepared us beforehand to understand that in this life on earth there will be trouble, tribulations and trials. Peter tells us that we shall be restored and made strong, firm and steadfast after we have suffered a little while.

As believers we are not exempt from encountering troubles. We shall suffer even after we have committed ourselves to the faith. James 1:3-4 tells us that when our faith is tested (by suffering), our endurance has a chance to grow and when our endurance is fully developed, we'll be complete, lacking nothing. This is the kind of restoration that God promises, and indeed gives us. We become strong in our faith, firm and steadfast so that we are unshakable and immovable.

> And the God of all grace, who called
> you to his eternal glory in Christ,
> after you have suffered a little while,
> will himself restore you and make
> you strong, firm and steadfast.
>
> (NIV)

1 Peter 1:7 says that the trials we face show that our faith is genuine and is being tested by fire just like gold is tested by fire. Since our faith is far more precious than gold, it must therefore withstand stronger fires than gold does and then come forth refined and pure. After all, as Paul stated in 1 Corinthians 3:13, on the judgment day our works will be tested by fire to determine if that work has value.

Therefore, we can expect suffering in the faith, as well as trials and tribulations. Let us then rejoice when our faith is tested because we know we will be restored to strength, firmness and steadfastness.

REFLECTIVE QUESTIONS

1 *Are you facing any testing or temptations in your life today?*

2 *Are you aware that Christ Jesus is able to restore you to strength and firmness to enable you withstand them?*

3 *How can you seek the Lord's preparation to enable you to withstand the testing by fire on judgment day?*

. . . .

Dear Lord, May I delight in you when temptations and testing come my way so that you may restore me to strength and firmness and so that my work may withstand the testing by fire when judgment day comes. Amen.

. . . .

My Reflections

Restored, strong, firm, and steadfast

2 Corinthians
5:14-17
(NKJV)

IN CHRIST, A NEW CREATION

God, in his faithful love for mankind, gave his one and only son to become human and to reconcile us to himself. Although he was God, Christ humbled himself and came down to earth, lived among us as a man, to the point of death on the cross to bear our sin and return us to the relationship that God initially envisioned and purposed between himself and mankind. This one man Christ died for all and if we choose to follow Christ and acknowledge Him as Saviour and Lord, we become a new creation. The old man diminishes and a new one arises in the spirit. Christ transforms our lives when we receive Him in our hearts and Isaiah 43:18-19 tells us to *"...not remember the former things, nor consider the things of old. Behold I will do a new thing, now it shall spring forth ..."* so we must then perceive in the spirit, the new thing the Lord is doing in our lives.

Since Christ died for us, once we are in him through faith, we are firmly reconciled to God. Upon reconciliation, we must forget our old selves

For the love of Christ compels us, because we judge
thus: that if one died for all, then all died; and He died
for all, that those who live should live no longer for
themselves, but for Him who died for them and rose
again. Therefore, from now on, we regard no one
according to the flesh. Even though we have known
Christ according to the flesh, yet now we know him
thus no longer. Therefore, if anyone is in Christ, he is a
new creation: old things have passed away; behold, all
things have become new.

(NKJV)

and forsake the things we used to do; we must set
our minds on godly things and abandon worldly
things to become the righteousness of God in Christ
and reflect God by Christ-like living. We must
be a changed people who are transformed by the
renewing of our minds so as to prove the good,
acceptable and perfect will of God as Paul stated in
Romans 12:2. We must also realize that God's love
towards us did not appear through any good works
we might have done, but according to his mercy he
saved us as Titus 3:5 tells us. We must put off our
former selves by the renewing of our minds and
instead put on the new self, created to be like God in
true righteousness and holiness (Ephesians 4:22).

How do we nurture this new being in us? By
no longer conforming to the ways of the world but
to the leading of God through the Holy Spirit. By
renewing our minds and attitudes. By seeking to
know him more each day through reading his word.
By consistently communicating with Him in prayer.
Our reward will come by relating with Him daily.

REFLECTIVE QUESTIONS

1. *Who or what do you live for?*
2. *Do you know the Lord Jesus as your Lord and Saviour?*
3. *How are embracing God's work at making you a new creation?*

. . . .

Lord, help me relate with you daily so that the new person in me can grow to maturity and so that I may become your righteousness in Christ. Amen.

. . . .

My Reflections

WHO NEEDS A DOCTOR?

Normally we won't find someone visiting a doctor when they are well and healthy. Some actually try to suppress or ignore any symptoms of illness to avoid visiting the doctor, earnestly hoping that the symptoms will go away and everything will return to normal. In fact for some, a visit to the doctor is one of those dreaded moments in our lives. Jesus echoed this reality while addressing the Pharisees and the scribes.

One day, Jesus decided to have dinner at Levi's house with tax collectors, people perceived as sinners, and his disciples. While there, the Pharisees and the scribes questioned why he ate with sinners and tax collectors. According to them, he should have only been socializing with his disciples and with them (pharisees and scribes) because they were the religious lot. They were the 'holy' ones who deserved a sitting with one who claimed to be from God. But Jesus' response was precise: the healthy do not need a doctor, the sick do. The righteous did not need him, but sinners did.

Jesus' mission was to reach out to sinners. And when he left, he commissioned us to do the same (Matthew 28:19-20; Luke 24:47).

How then has the church in our day become some sort of social club that enlists members with some commonness either in wealth, status, or education? How open are we as Christians to those who do not belong to the faith yet? And if we practice these Pharisaic attitudes and practices, how shall we then fulfil Jesus' mission and commission? Must we not dine with the tax collectors and "sinners" of our day? Must we not fellowship with the adulterous Samaritan woman over a drink as we reach out to her? Must we not also mingle with the Gentiles? How can we accomplish the great commission and reach the sinners as Jesus would?

We must follow the master's ways in our service to him. He has gone before us and has set the example so we have no choice but to follow that path lest we become like the Pharisees.

1   *What role are you playing in fulfilling the great commission?*

2   *Are you an enabler or a stumbling block for Christ's work unto salvation?*

3   *How can you reach out more effectively to the lost?*

. . . .

Dear Lord, help me follow your ways as I seek to fulfil the great commission. Amen.

. . . .

GROWTH

LET BOTH GROW TOGETHER

As believers we are the good seed in the field that God has planted. However, despite the fact that we are believers and belong to the kingdom of heaven, we are still placed in this sinful earth (John 17:14-16).

The master told the servants who had offered to remove the weeds from the field to let the weeds and the wheat grow together until harvest. As believers we will continue to grow amidst unbelievers including evil people who represent the weeds in the parable. Please notice that the response was specifically to *'let both grow together until harvest'* which means that both wheat and weed must grow to maturity since at harvest only mature plants are harvested. Those that don't weather the hard journey of growth do not reach maturity but are damaged along the way or dry up. This may happen due to too much heat that they cannot withstand or maybe they die because of lack of sufficient nutrients.

In our Christian life, we need to feed on the right food in order to derive the nutrients that will strengthen us and enable us thrive and grow to maturity and harvest (John 4:34; 17:17). Evildoers (represented by the weeds) are equally growing albeit in their evil. Believers and unbelievers grow together in equal measure on different growing lines and/or paths.

No wonder Jesus said in John 17:11 "...*but they are still in the world...protect them by the power of your name...*" In fact in verse 14 he says that he has "...*given them your word and the world has hated them, for they are not of the world any more than I am of the world...*" which means, like the wheat among which the master in the above parable allowed weeds to grow till harvest, Jesus has given His followers God's Word and they are not of the world, while also not taken out of the world. Verse 15 says, "...*my prayer is not that you take them out of the world but that you protect them from the evil one...*" See, we cannot be removed from the evil world or environment we live in, or from the evil offices that we work in, or from evil neighbourhoods, or even from evil families just because we are believers. God in his power will protect us but not necessarily remove us.

LET BOTH GROW TOGETHER

While we interact with those around us (our families, fellow countrymen, children, colleagues, business partners, neighbours), we must *"...have nothing to do with the fruitless deeds of darkness, but rather expose them..."* Ephesians 5:11. These '*deeds of darkness*' are happening all around us – we have not been removed from these environments, but God will protect us from the evil one.

In 2 Corinthians 6:14-18, Paul warns us against being *"...yoked together with unbelievers. For what do righteousness and wickedness have in common? Or what fellowship can light have with darkness?... Therefore, "come out from them and be separate, says the Lord. Touch no unclean thing and I will receive you."* (NIV). Here we also see the emphasis on the fact that we are all together in this journey of life - believers and unbelievers. We are called to shine Christ's light among unbelievers. 'Not being yoked together' means we cannot do what they are doing, we cannot be partners in their growth, we cannot be in harmony with them because we are different. Wheat and weeds are very different.

In Matthew 13:47-50, Jesus likened the kingdom of heaven to a net let down into the lake which caught all kinds of fish. He goes on to say, *"...When it was full, the fishermen pulled it up on the shore. Then they sat down and collected the good fish in baskets but threw the bad away. This is how it will be at the end of the age. The angels will come and separate the wicked from the righteous and throw them into the blazing furnace..."* (NIV)

The hard reality is that God allows good and evil to grow together and separation only happens at harvest. The question is, how are you standing in your faith? Are you being light and salt in your surroundings? How is your walk with the Lord? Have you conformed to the standards of this world or are you being transformed by the renewing of your mind? What do you feed on to help you grow in the right direction ready for the harvest?

REFLECTIVE QUESTIONS

1. *Are you a follower of Christ?*
2. *Are you feeding on the right nourishment and growing in the right direction?*
3. *When separation comes, will you remain on the Lord's side or will you be thrown into the blazing furnace?*

. . . .

Lord, please help me in my journey of growth so that I can feed on nutritious spiritual food and grow in the right direction so that at the time of harvest, I may remain at your side as the wicked are thrown into the blazing furnace. Amen

. . . .

A PROPHET WITHOUT HONOUR

Jesus himself acknowledges that prophets have honour but not in their own town, among their relatives or in their own home. This should serve to encourage those of us who are believers in homes where no one else is Christian. We must be ready to be rejected, despised, and even humiliated for our affiliation with Christ. We are not peculiar. If the Master was not accepted by the people, who had all along been waiting for the Messiah, then we as his followers should also not expect acceptance.

We should not be discouraged but rather this should serve to encourage us and spur us on to the course that we have been called by Christ. We are to be like him, to reflect and glorify him with our lives. Now that we bear his mark on our lives, others must wonder where we get the things we do and say. Others must wonder whether we are not just the 'ordinary other' that they know and they indeed must take offense at us as they took offense at him (*Mark 6:3*). If they are comfortable with who we are then we have a problem.

What must worry us, however, is when they are comfortable with us and our way of doing things. We must be different. We must do things differently in our environments that might make people uncomfortable. We must be different from our siblings who are not believers. We must be different from our colleagues who are not believers. We must be different from our business partners who have not encountered the Lord Jesus Christ. **WE MUST BE DIFFERENT** from those that are not believers in Christ. We must be different in a godly manner. Paul challenges us to be separate for the Lord to receive us. (2 Cor. 6:16-17). Jesus says that we are not of the world any more than he is (John 17:14-16) and therefore, we must be different to reflect where we belong.

1 *Have you been transformed and conformed to Christ's likeness?*

2 *Do people see Christ in you?*

3 *Do you seek honour and respect from people instead of following Christ?*

....

Lord, help me to be more like you every single day of my life. May I do things that are from you that others may even wonder whether it's the me they know and wonder from where I got these things from. May I be comfortable to be without honour in my own town, home and family for your sake. Amen.

....

My Reflections

A prophet without honour

WHAT ARE YOU SOWING?

Do not deceived:
God cannot
be mocked.
A man reaps
what he sows.
(NIV)

Luke 8:4-8 (Parable of the sower)

When we think about sowing, we think of the farmers who work so hard during planting season, striving to beat the rains and so benefit from them. These farmers, however, don't just wake up one morning and sow. They take time to prepare their land; they invest money to pay labourers who till the soil; they invest money to buy the seed for sowing and they invest their time in all these undertakings. In all these preparations, those who prepare well will not be caught off guard.

However, preparation is not all that counts when sowing time comes, whatever one sows will determine what will be harvested. It is also important to plan where to plant as reflected in the parable of the sower. You cannot just throw your seeds anywhere and expect a bumper crop.

In our lives, we are like the farmers, constantly having opportunities to sow seed. And though we may imagine, especially in the Christian church context, that sowing relates to financial giving, that is not the only way we plant seeds. We can sow in many forms whether it's by giving our time, or our expertise, or money, or property or most importantly giving of ourselves to Christ.

Sometimes we might wonder where or what to give and so we just sit back. Yet opportunities are all around us and the Lord is waiting for us to respond. We can visit a sick neighbour or stranger who needs encouragement. How about that prayer or Bible study group that needs a venue to fellowship – can you open your house up to them? Then there might be a needy child in the public school in your neighbourhood who has no one to pay for

Give and it will be given to you. A good measure, pressed down, shaken together and running over, will be poured into your lap. For with the measure you use, it will be measured to you. (NIV)

WHAT ARE YOU SOWING?

his school meals – is the Lord looking to you to respond? How about the grannie in the old people's home who needs food supplies for the week – you can plant your seed there. And those seats in your church that always need cleaning so people can enjoy ministry on Sunday – go clean them.

There are many opportunities to serve the Lord in our environment and in so doing we are sowing. When the harvest time comes we'll surely enjoy a bumper harvest if we sow generously as the Bible tells us. If we sow generosity, kindness, peace, encouragement and all the virtuous seeds, we will reap a virtuous harvest, but if we sow meanness, rudeness, jealousy and all the evil seeds, that is what we will reap. Beware of what you are sowing, because harvest time is coming.

REFLECTIVE QUESTIONS

1. *What, how and where in your life do you sow – money, time, talent or whatever else you are sowing?*
2. *Did you realize that what you'll harvest will be proportional to what you have sowed?*
3. *Are you a generous sower?*

Lord, I desire to sow generously. I desire to sow in fertile soil and not in rocks and thorns. Lord, help me to give so that it can come back to me in good measure, pressed down and spilling over because I know you are not mocked and whatever I sow, that I shall reap. Amen.

My Reflections

OBEDIENCE

OBEDIENCE IS BETTER THAN SACRIFICE

The act of obeying the Lord, which is better than sacrifice, causes God's glory or his glorious presence to fill our lives beyond human comprehension. His presence is there to lead our way and to cover us day and night. At times we are quick to offer sacrifices to God and yet we do not follow his commands in obedience. We imagine or assume that God so values and appreciates our efforts that he will not remember that we have not obeyed His word. It almost seems that we are trying to bribe God.

Our sacrifice is represented by the works we do for God or the service we offer. Do you work hard to serve God and sacrifice to Him in ministry? For instance, singing for him, leading worship, leading Bible study, serving in church leadership, teaching Sunday school, playing instruments in church, going for outreach and missions, ushering worshippers into church on Sunday – or whatever other ministry you take part in as an individual. It is great that you are serving the Lord in these capacities, however, if you do all or any of these while you do not obey God, then your sacrifice is worth nothing in his presence. In fact, 1 Samuel 15:23 says that rebellion or disobedience are like the sin of witchcraft.

Some people serve so diligently in those roles, however, they are not obedient to God in many other ways – their lives may be full of deceitfulness or sexual immorality, they are scornful, selfish, hateful, drunkards, full of envy, jealous and any of the other acts of the flesh outlined in Galatians 5:19.

Many blessings are promised to us if we obey the Lord's commands as we see in Leviticus 26:3-13. These blessings would not come if they sacrificed the best of offerings but only if they obeyed his commands.

Before you think about what you will offer to the Lord in the form of sacrifice, consider your obedience or disobedience to him, because to God obedience is better than sacrifice.

> **Proverbs 21:3**
>
> To do righteousness and justice is more acceptable to the Lord than sacrifice.

1   *Do you value sacrificing to God more than obeying his commands?*

2   *Did you realize that obeying God has to be complete, you cannot obey in bits and pieces?*

3   *How can you increase your obedience to God?*

Dear Lord, teach my heart to obey you always. May what I offer you as sacrifice always be accompanied with obedience. Amen.

My Reflections

IN YOUR POSITION FOR SUCH A TIME AS THIS

Often it is easy to forget those who may be suffering because we think we have entered a place of safety and that the circumstances they are encountering are far removed from our own lives. As humans we easily forget where we have come from, how we got here and who brought us here.

Esther's story is one of pain. Having lost her parents early in life, her cousin Mordecai adopted her and brought her up as his own. Mordecai's great concern and mindfulness of Esther is evident when the king's edict to summon virgins from all the 127 provinces was given and Mordecai brought her to be among those to be considered by King Xerxes to replace Queen Vashti.

God's ways are mysterious and Esther received favour from the king's officials, the eunuchs and even the king himself – and she was crowned queen.

Much later, Mordecai displeased Haman who convinced the king that there was a people group who do not respect and honour him and therefore an edict was issued to annihilate all the Jews in the land of Persia. At this point, Queen Esther needs to act to save them even at the risk of her own life. When she expressed her hesitation, Mordecai rebuked her and encouraged her to do everything in her power to seek the king's favour.

What was God's agenda in allowing Esther to become queen at such a time and in such a kingdom? We might say in today's language that the Jews were like refugees or asylum seekers. They had no status, no citizenship and no residency, and yet God allowed the Jewish girl, Esther, to become queen. God's divine purpose was at the centre of this story with his beloved people of Israel. When it was time to carry out the divine agenda, Esther was unaware of God's purpose and concern that she couldn't do what was expected. These were purely human requirements, plans and procedures but our God is not bound by human limitations, or restricted by human plans and procedures. He's not constrained or bound by human laws. He is God. He is over all. He is in control of all. He works in his own way.

God's plan is always in place for his glory and therefore if you are part of the cast in his plan, be attentive and alert lest you miss out on your role. Who knows but that you may be in your position for such a time as this?

REFLECTIVE QUESTIONS

1   *What role are you playing in the position that God has placed you today?*

2   *Are you daily tuned to God to get his instructions?*

3   *If you fail to obey God's direction, he'll still accomplish his purpose through someone or something else and you will miss out on the blessing. How can you ensure that you are attentive to God's direction?*

. . . .

Lord, help me to play my rightful role in my family, workplace, nation, church or wherever you place me. May I daily be tuned to you in today's very noisy environment so that I may understand the times and thus deliberately and informatively play my God-given role. Amen.

. . . .

A STIFF-NECKED PEOPLE

Have you ever trusted someone for a period of time and then in the midst of your long waiting you become impatient and doubtful and you wonder whether they remember you are still waiting for them? For instance, you are meant to take a trip somewhere and a friend promises you a ride but doesn't show up when expected and in fact tells you they are held up in traffic, or in a meeting that doesn't seem to end, or that they are in a supermarket picking up something quick. But time keeps on ticking and they don't arrive and you conclude that they are lying to you and not coming, or else something has happened to them and thus they may not show up. You then decide to take off in a different direction, or return home, or use alternate means to get to your destination.

This is what the Israelites did when Moses was so long in coming down from the mountain where he was meeting the Lord. They discussed among themselves and with Aaron concluding that they had no idea what had happened to 'that fellow Moses' and he probably wasn't coming back. Their faltering faith, their impatience and finally digression was accounted to them as stiff-neckedness by God himself. In his anger he threatened to destroy them and start over with a new nation through Moses.

God hates our unbelief. When we doubt his love, his power, his grace, or his word it displeases him. And who can stand his anger? Our unbelief is equivalent to disobedience and disobedience will cause us to perish (Hebrews 4:11). Although God is stern in his operations and rules, if we are receptive to his kindness and grace unto salvation, we'll be grafted into him. If we continue in unbelief, however, we shall be cut off (Romans 11:20-23). If our faith is weak we might doubt God's promises but if our faith is firm and strong, it shall be accounted to us as righteousness just as for Abraham (Romans 4:19-25). If we hear God's word and instruction and disobey, it is accounted to us as unbelief (Hebrews 3:16-19).

Let us therefore desire to obey God's commands. Our obedience begins with our faith in Him in everything that He says and has promised through His word. And when our faith seems to falter and to give up, let us seek His help.

REFLECTIVE QUESTIONS

1   *Do you at times find it difficult to hold on to your faith?*

2   *Are you ever confronted with so many contradictions in your environment that waiting for God becomes really difficult?*

3   *Who is in your surroundings and what are they influencing you to do as you wait for God? How can you ensure that you will wait faithfully as you serve God?*

. . . .

Lord, at times it's not easy to hold on to faith in you in the midst of so much doubt and many contradictions all around me. I pray that you help my unbelief when the temptation to lose my faith beckons. Amen.

. . . .

OBEY YOUR SPIRITUAL LEADERS

Our spiritual leaders and indeed all leaders are chosen of God. While this may be hard to understand, the Bible tells us that God permits or allows them to be in those positions of leadership and power.

When the Israelites pressured Samuel to give them a king in order to be like all the other nations around them, God allowed Saul to become king over them (1 Samuel 8). In those days, the king also served as a spiritual leader and could therefore petition God on behalf of the people as well as prophesy.

Often people tend to defy not only the spiritual leaders they assume not to have been chosen by God but also those that they recognize to have been explicitly chosen by God (Exodus 32:1-4; Joshua 7:10-26). When those leaders stand for what the people themselves don't stand for, they may defy their call.

In all these instances, when the people defied or disobeyed the spiritual leaders he had placed over them, God counted it as disobedience to himself and not to the human leaders. In 1 Samuel 8:7, the Lord told Samuel that, "...*it is not you they have rejected, but they* have rejected me as their king...” In Exodus 32:8, God says, *“they have been quick to turn away from what I commanded them and have made themselves an idol cast in the shape of a calf...”* In Joshua 7:11, the Lord told Joshua that, *“Israel has sinned; they have violated my covenant, which I commanded them to keep...”*

Spiritual leaders over us bear God's authority in our lives. We must therefore be careful how we treat their instruction lest the Lord's anger burn against us for our disobedience. We must be alert to how we respond to their instruction and direction. Do we make them watch over our souls with joy or with pain? Do we burden them with sorrow and grief or do we make their ministry light and enjoyable? Do we esteem them highly in love for the sake of their work or do we dishonour and disrespect them? Whatever we do in response to our spiritual leaders, may it only be beneficial and profitable for ministry and to the glory of God.

1 Thessalonians 5:12-13

Now we ask you, brothers and sisters, to acknowledge those who work hard among you, who care for you in the Lord and who admonish you. Hold them in the highest regard in love because of their work. Live in peace with each other.
(NIV)

1. *Do you have confidence in your spiritual leaders?*
2. *Do you submit to their authority?*
3. *How can you show respect to your leaders?*

. . . .

Lord, help me to respect and esteem your servants whom you have appointed as leaders over my life for the sake of ministry. Amen.

. . . .

WORSHIP

A SWEET AROMA TO THE LORD

I love perfume. In fact, I cherish pure and unadulterated perfume. Authentic perfume has such amazing and refreshing scents that can indeed turn a dull day into a super bright one. Smelling good pure perfume actually makes you happy.

In Leviticus chapters 1-4, we see clear guidelines from God to the children of Israel through his servant Moses on how to worship him. Worship through sacrifice is the key since he is a holy God. In this passage we see God requiring the Israelites to sacrifice, for example, 'a male without blemish' – Leviticus 1:3, 10. One could also offer birds or grain offerings. God emphasized that the burnt offerings must be 'without blemish', 'fine flour' and 'a sweet aroma to the Lord'.

We all have different gifts and circumstances and pass through a variety of challenges. Our trials are varied because we are all running a race in different lanes. Therefore, the sacrifices that we bring to God are different and as represented in

Leviticus 1-4, all these offerings and sacrifices are acceptable to God. It doesn't matter what the other person brings as their sacrifice, God does not expect the same from all of us. Just as there are different scents of perfume, so there are different kinds of sacrifices. However, whatever your sacrifice of worship, once made to the Lord, it must be an offering that produces a sweet aroma, pleasing to the Lord.

Romans 12:1 urges us to present our bodies as a living sacrifice, holy and acceptable to God. Whatever trials and tribulations our physical bodies go through, they must in the end be presentable to God as a living sacrifice of worship. They must be 'not contaminated' by any worldly effects. Our bodies must be devoid of sin: our mouths/tongues in what we say, our ears in what we listen to, our hands in what we touch, our feet in where we go, our eyes in

1 Peter

2:5

You also, like living stones, are being built into a spiritual house to be a holy priesthood, offering spiritual sacrifices acceptable to God through Jesus Christ. (NIV)

A SWEET AROMA TO THE LORD

what we look at, our minds in what we think about, and our hearts in what we love. The wholesomeness of our bodies must be without blemish. They must produce a sweet aroma to the Lord offered as a sacrifice of worship every day. Therefore, our everyday lifestyle must conform to the laws of God and not of the world.

In 1 Peter 2:5, we are referred to as living stones built up as a spiritual house and we are a holy priesthood called to offer spiritual sacrifices acceptable to God through Jesus Christ. Our lives are in focus again, required to be offered as spiritual sacrifices that are acceptable to God.

We must also do it continually as worship cannot and should not be a one-off affair. Worshipping God should be a lifestyle, a way of life, our first nature. Hebrews 13:15 tells us to *"...continually offer the sacrifice of praise to God, that is the fruit of our lips..."*

All we have to remember is that our offering of worship must be a sweet aroma to the Lord. We therefore must work every day to eliminate any foul thing in our lives lest it contaminates our sacrifice to God.

REFLECTIVE QUESTIONS

1   *Do you know that your praise is a sacrifice to God?*

2   *Is your life clean or contaminated?*

3   *How is your life producing a sweet aroma to the Lord?*

. . . .

Dear God, help me live a life worthy of your name and as I offer myself every day as a living sacrifice, may that offering be a sweet aroma to you. Amen.

. . . .

WHAT DOES YOUR SACRIFICE TO THE LORD COST?

Hebrews
10:14

For by one sacrifice he has made perfect forever those who are being made holy.
(NIV)

Some of us serve the Lord in church, others in leadership of government and private institutions. Regardless of where we are serving the Lord, we must give of ourselves to that service. We must consciously be aware that we are serving him, if we really are. Our service in whatever capacity becomes our sacrifice to the Lord which costs us something: our time, our skill, our effort, our energy, our intellect, our physical input, our finances, our jobs, our children, our comfort, our spouses or our friendship.

By giving His only Son, Jesus, God gave one grand and sufficient sacrifice that has earned us eternity with him. God himself demonstrated that a worthy sacrifice has a cost. When Abraham was about to sacrifice his only son Isaac, God stopped him and presented a ram for sacrifice. Abraham thus demonstrated that he was willing to sacrifice to God the most valued and precious gift he had in his life. In fact it appears he did not even stop to wonder how all the promises God had made to him that were to come to pass through Isaac would eventually come to pass. His act demonstrated his faith.

While serving God and offering our sacrifices, we might face tribulation from the evil one, we might encounter persecution from friends or enemies, we might be deserted, or ridiculed, we might lose jobs or business opportunities, fail exams or much more. Our sacrifices to God cost us something.

If we only serve the Lord during our free time, that sacrifice costs us nothing, after all we were free and hence we're just killing time. If we only give our finances when we have extra in our pockets, that sacrifice costs us nothing. 2 Cor. 8:2-3 tells us of the Macedonian church where people, despite their many troubles and great

By faith Abraham, when God tested him, offered Isaac as a sacrifice. He who had embraced the promises was about to sacrifice his one and only son. (NIV)

poverty, overflowed in rich generosity and gave not only what they could afford but far more. Whatever we are offering to the Lord must cost us something.

Once we have offered our gifts and sacrifices to the Lord, we shall pray as in Psalm 20:3 that the Lord remembers all our sacrifices and accepts our offerings.

REFLECTIVE QUESTIONS

1   *Do you realize that the sacrifices you offer to God are important to Him?*
2   *How much do your sacrifices to God cost you?*
3   *Do you offer to God sacrifices that are worthy of His name?*

Dear God, help me recognize that the sacrifices I offer are important to you and therefore they must cost me something to be worthy of your name. May I learn not to offer to you sacrifices that cost me nothing. Amen.

My Reflections

THANKFUL IN ALL CIR-CUMSTANCES

Paul directed the Thessalonians to be joyful, to never stop praying, and to be thankful in all circumstances. We notice that the instruction is not to be thankful for all circumstances. Not every circumstance in our life warrants thankfulness. Though it is difficult, it is not impossible to thank God even when we are in the midst of trials that we are not thankful for. While you are in that awful circumstance, that discouraging circumstance that is draining your faith and energy, that journey of ill health, while you are dealing with that failing relationship, when you are going through that divorce or when you are mourning the loss of a loved one, whatever circumstance you are in, be thankful to God not for it but for the truth of who God is in the midst of it.

In challenging seasons, it's easy for our focus to dwell on the ill that is troubling us. But you know what, amidst that trouble, in the course of that bad season, as we struggle through that difficulty, there are many 'small' miracles that exist and if we deliberately choose to look for and focus on those, we'll be thankful in bad as well as in good circumstances.

> Always be joyful. Never
> stop praying. Be thankful in
> all circumstances, for this
> is God's will for you who
> belong to Christ Jesus.
> (NLT)

Although it's painful to lose a loved one, when going through the loss, we can thank God for the gift of the person for the time we had them in our lives. When you grieve the loss of that job that enabled you to pay your bills, thank God for His supply of that same job while it lasted and even thank him for his provision in the days ahead. In fact just thank God for He is God and our circumstances do not change who He is.

REFLECTIVE QUESTIONS

1   *Do you at times find yourself in circumstances so difficult that it is hard to be thankful?*

2   *How can you seek God's grace to enable you be thankful even when you are going through difficult circumstances?*

Dear God, It is not easy to always be thankful. I pray that you empower me to thank you in whatever circumstances I face and to trust you always just because you are God. Amen.

PURE AND UNDEFILED RELIGION

A friend of mine who had not yet met the Lord had just moved into a new neighbourhood and was looking for a church. One day she decided to visit a church which was very near to her house. When she reached the entrance, an usher welcomed her in. But just before she could make her way completely through the door, that same usher tapped her on the shoulder in the company of another usher and whispered to her, "This is a really pretty dress but it's quite short for church." At that moment my friend thought, "I just need to get out of here and go back home." But she decided to stay, after all she had left her house to come and look for God and she was going to stay despite the unpleasant incident. Throughout the service, however, she could not really pay attention to what was happening as she was distracted by that experience at the entrance. When the service ended that day she went home but never returned to that church. In fact, she did not go to any other church for a year due to that one experience.

How many times do we serve as closed doors at church, busy blocking souls that are earnestly and desperately searching for God, from reaching the God we say we serve? We act as if we are keeping guard for God yet he is able to keep guard for himself. Remember when Peter cut off the ear of one of the soldiers who came to arrest Jesus before the crucifixion – what did Jesus do? He asked Peter to put his sword away and in fact added that he was able to ask the Father to defend him (John 18:10-11; Matthew 26:51-53). Jesus was telling Peter and everybody else present that he was able to sort out his own issues. He is well able to guard his territory when needed. How many times do we cause hungry and thirsty souls to stumble right at the place where they are meant to come and find God and find rest for their souls? All this in the name of the religion that we are trying to safeguard and preserve.

We often apply our misadvised human standards in defining what true religion is. We set the rules and regulations against which everyone is measured to determine their religiosity and 'godliness'. Little

PURE AND UNDEFILED RELIGION

do we understand these are just human standards - our rules and not God's. We think that true religion is merely doing church every Sunday but God's view is different (James 1:27). We have convinced ourselves that our outward appearance is what defines how religious we are, yet God looks at the heart (1 Samuel 16:7). We must constantly remind ourselves that our own righteousness is like filthy rags and so it is not fitting in God's presence (Isaiah 64:6). Our thoughts are so far from his thoughts and our ways from his ways that we cannot of ourselves define to others what God's standards are, but we must make reference to his word on what his ways and standards are (Isaiah 55:8-9). No wonder Jesus dared the Scribes and the Pharisees, who presented to him the woman caught in adultery, to be the first to throw a stone at her if they had no sin. They all walked away until only Jesus was left with the woman.

As we stand at the doors and gates of church to block those we think should not get in and to let in those that in our eyes deserve entry, what does God the Father expect of us? When we stand on that pulpit to speak, do our words minister life or death, do they draw close or repel those that earnestly seek God?

In fact, according to God, true religion is simple and far removed from what we think it is. God expects us to visit orphans and widows in their trouble. He expects us to love our neighbour as ourselves and indeed to love our enemies. God is not assigning us to be guards at his gates to block unwanted people. We are not appointed to watch out for and keep sinners from reaching him (Luke 18:15-16).

REFLECTIVE QUESTIONS

1. *What is religion to you?*
2. *What do you think religion from God's perspective is?*
3. *Ask God to reveal his expectations for you in regard to religion?*

Dear God, guide me and direct me to practice true religion in your eyes. May I be careful not to set or even follow the standards of men but always seek to understand what your purpose is. Amen.

My Reflections

SERVICE

DO NOT DEPART FROM THE TEMPLE

If you are like me, at times in your life you wonder what is happening to you or even what direction your life is taking. When undesirable, difficult and unexpected circumstances catch up with me, I am tempted to go and find some happiness and fun; we call it unwinding. When I am looking for a job and I am not successful, when I sit an exam and fail, when I give a shot at a business deal and it doesn't seem to be working, when a good friend betrays me, when dealing with a sick child, sibling or parent, the pressure mounts and mounts and mounts. At some point, I just want to go out and have coffee with a good friend, I want to go swimming and just let go as I enjoy a good swim, I want to make merry with a friend or maybe even take a holiday to the beach to divert my mind from the difficulty and to alleviate the prevailing pressure, even if for a while.

It was not so for prophetess Anna. Luke 2:37b says '...*She did not depart from the temple, worshipping with fasting and prayer night and day...*' And in that temple, the Messiah found her when He was presented to Simeon for purification.

Anna the prophetess got married and lived seven years with her husband until she was widowed. We are told that after that she did not depart from the temple, worshipping with fasting and prayer night and day. Amazing! She lived in the temple worshipping with fasting and prayer. Night and day.

What an amazing life choice for a woman who, humanly speaking could have been elsewhere doing something else. She did not seem to pity herself for losing a husband so soon after marriage or for not having children or for not finding a new husband. Amazingly, Anna chose to stay in the temple and took on the occupation of worship, with fasting and prayer. We can only imagine how many things she fasted and prayed about. She must have interceded for so many people in her day.

Evidently, praying and waiting for the Messiah were on the top on her list because verse 38 says that, *"And coming up at that very hour she began to give thanks to God and to speak of him to all who were*

DO NOT DEPART FROM THE TEMPLE

waiting for the redemption of Jerusalem," when Jesus' parents brought him to Jerusalem to present him to the Lord in accordance with the law of Moses.

The description of this prophetess fits in just three verses. Yet, they are weighty. We know that she did not depart from the temple; we know that she worshipped with fasting and prayer night and day; and we also know that she beheld Christ (the Messiah).

How blessed it is to devote a life to worshipping God and then God indeed honours you with a gift you did not expect. Her life of devotion was not in vain. She not only beheld Jesus but received the revelation that he was the Messiah and she was able to speak of him to all who were waiting for the redemption of Jerusalem.

Beloved, do not depart from the temple, do not quit worshipping the Most High because even though he tarries, he shall surely come through for you. The waiting time doesn't matter, keep waiting, keep praying and keep watching out for him. You may not dwell literally in the temple like Anna did but do not depart from God's presence; devote your life to worshipping and serving the Lord because it is in his presence that we find fullness of joy, in his presence are pleasures evermore, in his presence the Messiah will find you and you shall behold your blessing.

1   *How are you serving the Lord?*

2   *Do you realize that as you serve and wait faithfully the Lord will grant your heart's desires?*

· ·

Lord, help me to keep at your service in your presence even as I wait for you. Amen.

· ·

GENUINE BROKENNESS

Often times, our history informs our present and our future. This not only happens in our ordinary lives but also in our spiritual journey. Many times, what our past was, determines the kind of spiritual life we lead today. In fact, if we had such a sinful past, we may tend to be held captive and are unable to fully give of ourselves completely to serving the Lord as we should. At times our family background is what holds us back. Other times the environment we find ourselves in just puts us so down that we cannot serve as we ought. We are not peculiar, others who have gone before us encountered similar circumstances.

Our scripture of reference gives an account of a sinful woman who showed up where Jesus had been invited by some Pharisees, with a jar of perfume. *Verse 37-38 – And behold, a woman in the city who was a sinner, when she knew that Jesus sat at the table in the Pharisee's house, brought an alabaster flask of fragrant oil, and stood at His feet behind Him weeping; and she began to wash His feet with her tears, and wiped them with the hair of her head;*

and she kissed His feet and anointed them with the fragrant oil. When she came, she stood behind him weeping, washing his feet with her tears, wiping them with her hair and anointing them with the perfume that she had brought. At that, the Pharisees found good reason to further doubt Jesus since they wondered how, if he was a prophet, could not even know that the woman who was touching him was such a sinner.

However, Jesus, knowing their thoughts, told them that the woman had done what none of them had done to him since he came into the house. Verse 44-46 – *"Then He turned to the woman and said to Simon, "Do you see this woman? I entered your house; you gave Me no water for My feet, but she has washed my feet with her tears and wiped them with the hair of her head. You gave Me no kiss, but this woman has not ceased to kiss My feet since the time I came in. You did not anoint My head with oil, but this woman has anointed My feet with fragrant oil. Therefore I say to you, her sins, which are many, are forgiven, for she loved much. But to whom little is forgiven, the same*

GENUINE BROKENNESS

loves little." In fact, he told them that she had done a good work for him and that wherever the gospel would be preached, her story would also be told. That tells us that Jesus approved and was indeed touched by her brokenness and genuine service to him. It did not matter what the Pharisees thought about her and in fact it did not matter what her past really was like. What mattered was what she decided to do in His presence. She did not let the environment keep her away from her act of service and worship, she did not yield to her sinful past. He brokenness in service and worship inside the Pharisee's house moved the Lord and that's why her story is in the gospel.

Is your past a dark one? Is your family background and history unpleasant? Does your academic profile look shameful? Is your social environment harsh, hostile or judgmental? What is it that colours or shades your life? What is it that holds you back from genuinely breaking in the presence of the Master and giving him genuine service and worship? You can lay it off. You can unfocus from the negative environment and only focus on the Lord. He pays attention to your genuine service and worship to Him. He does not pay attention to those who are busy accusing you before him – including the devil (Job 1:6-11). He does not focus on those who are busy judging you based on your past. He is focusing on you and awaits your broken service and worship to Him.

REFLECTIVE QUESTIONS

1. *Did you know that Jesus does not focus on what others are reporting to him about you?*
2. *What in your life holds you back from genuinely serving and worshiping God as you ought?*
3. *Did you know that God awaits you to get genuinely broken in his presence and that He desires that you worship Him?*

. . . .

Dear God, help me to unfocus from the things in my life that hold me back from breaking in your presence and serving you as I ought. May I only focus on pleasing you and touching your heart regardless of my environment or my past. Amen.

. . . .

THE BOOK OF MEMORABLE DEEDS

At times it seems natural to do good and at other times we struggle and need some incentive. We look for motivation and encouragement. At times, we even want recognition in order to do what is good. But more often than not, our good deeds are not noticed or recognized, let alone rewarded and at that point we may want to quit doing more good. Seldom are our good deeds recorded in the book of memorable deeds.

But we should not get tired of doing what is good. As Paul stated in Galatians *6:9 "...And let us not grow weary of doing good, for in due season, we will reap, if we do not give up." (ESV)*

So keep at it. Keep doing the works of faith God has given you to do and in due time, you will be remembered. In Esther 6:1, we are told of a night when *"...the king could not sleep. And he gave orders to bring the book of memorable deeds, the chronicles, and they were read before the king."* And that was the beginning of big things for Mordecai and the entire Jewish community. Plans turned upside down for Haman and things worked out as no one could have imagined for Mordecai. All because of his good deeds which were recorded in the book of memorable deeds. Thus the King remembered them and rewarded Mordecai.

Are you lying there as Mordecai at the King's gate, forgotten and desperate? Is it hard to see how this can end well? Cheer up and rejoice because the book of memorable deeds is still before the King of Kings and soon he's going to give orders that it be brought and read before him. All your deeds will be brought to his mind. All your good deeds of faith will be read out. And in that day, the King will delight to honour you. Hallelujah! So, keep on doing good; it will be recorded and your day of honour is coming. Your Father who sees what is done in secret will reward you (Matthew 6:4b) and He will prepare a table before you in the presence of your enemies (Psalm 23:5).

1   *Have you been doing any good deeds which no one is noticing?*

2   *Do you feel tired and worn out and even want to quit doing what is good?*

3   *Are you aware that one day all your good deeds will be brought to remembrance and read out?*

....

Dear God, grant me the patience to keep doing good in faith and may the book of memorable deeds one day be read out to you and may you in that day delight to honour me in the presence of my enemy. Amen.

....

My Reflections

THE SHEPHERD MUST TAKE RESPONSIBILITY

**1 Chronicles 21
2 Samuel 24:1-24**

Joab the commander of the army carried out the king's order. Although he did not believe in what the king wanted done, he still obeyed and went throughout the land counting the people. After nine months and 20 days, they returned to the king with the count – 800,000 men in Israel and 500,000 in Judah.

No sooner had David gotten his desire than his heart condemned him and he called to the Lord saying, *"I have sinned greatly in what I have done; but now I pray, O Lord, take away the iniquity of your servant for I have done very foolishly."*

The Lord must have looked at David and thought to himself, foolish man! I sent you warnings but you did not pay attention! Now here you are. But God is forever merciful (Lamentations 3:22-23) and he therefore paid attention to David. He gave three options for David to choose from in verse 13:

So the King said to Joab the commander of the army who was with him, "Now go throughout all the tribes of Israel, from Dan to Beersheba, and count the people, that I may know the number of the people." And Joab said to the king, "...but why does my lord the king desire this thing? ...nevertheless, the king's word prevailed against Joab and against the captains of the army...."

i) *Shall seven years of famine come to you in your land?*

ii) *Shall you flee three months before your enemies while they pursue you?*

iii) *Shall there be three days' plague in your land?*

So David chose to fall into the Lord's hand and not man's for he reckoned that the Lord is merciful. And the Lord sent the plague and seventy thousand people died as a result. It must have been painful.

David was aware that he had caused this punishment and he spoke to the Lord when he saw the angel of the Lord striking the people. Verse 17 says, *"surely I have sinned, and I have done wickedly; but these sheep, what have they done? Let your hand, I pray, be against me and against my father's house"*

What a loss! What a heavy price to pay! But fortunately David eventually came to his senses and took responsibility as the shepherd who was causing all this suffering and death.

THE SHEPHERD MUST TAKE RESPONSIBILITY

At times the decisions we take when in positions of leadership seem right in our minds. It may be at work, in our church ministry, in our families, or in our business ventures. We do not want to listen to the advice of the experts the Lord has placed in our path – remember David's words prevailed against Joab's.

No matter what, though, we have to be ready to take responsibility for the consequences of our actions. Some of the consequences hit hard and heavy. And in this we must act fast lest the sheep suffer under God's wrath because of our inaction. Most importantly we should think through our decisions carefully and prayerfully before we translate them into actions that might be sinful and painful. May the Lord help us to be alert and sensitive to His Spirit.

REFLECTIVE QUESTIONS

1   *Are you in a position of authority where you often ignore advisors' wisdom?*

2   *Are you aware that God can at times speak to you through an advisor or your junior or servant?*

3   *When you make the wrong decision as a leader, are you quick to take responsibility and remedy the situation?*

. . . .

Dear Lord, guide me in every decision that I make especially where that decision affects the lives of other people. When I miss your guidance at the decision making stage, may I be quick to take responsibility even when consequences come hitting hard. Amen.

. . . .

CHRIST'S AMBASSADORS

Ambassadors in other countries represent their country's government. In fact, you hardly see or look at any ambassador as an individual as long as he or she is in a representational role for their government. This means we look at an ambassador through the lens of the government represented. The ambassador automatically represents the values, ideologies, principles and standards of that government.

An ambassador also negotiates any deals for their government with the country where they have been sent and communicates government positions to the host country. No matter what personal opinions or ideas they may have, it is important to stand with the government's position.

Like these earthly ambassadors, we who have been reconciled to God through Christ are ambassadors for him and as Paul puts it, it is as though God is pleading through us for the world's reconciliation to him. We must represent Christ's kingdom and government in this "country" that hosts us for now. We must speak for heaven's values, we must stand for heaven's ideologies and ideas, we must represent heaven's standards, and we must reflect heaven's position in all we do.

As ambassadors for Christ, when people look at us, they must recognize and acknowledge heaven and not us. When we speak, we must do so in a manner that people recognize who we speak for. We must concern ourselves only with business that concerns our government and only negotiate deals that our government has sent us to negotiate, because we are not our own but were bought at a price (1 Corinthians 6:19-20).

As Christians in this age, what do we represent? Whose position do we take on issues? Are we conformed to the standards of this world while compromising the standards of the government we represent? Can we stand to be counted as representatives of God in this troubled world today? The challenge is real but the commission has not changed. We must represent the government that has commissioned us as ambassadors and we must only stand by its position on all matters. There's no room for wavering or compromise.

REFLECTIVE QUESTIONS

1   *Did you know you are a foreigner and an exile on this earth?*

2   *Whose position and interests do you represent in your environment?*

3   *As an ambassador for Christ, how can you reflect the values of heaven while on this earth?*

Dear God, as an ambassador for Christ, I desire to represent only your position and your heavenly values while I am on this earth. I ask that you would empower me and enable me to work for you and to reflect your righteousness through Christ in me. Amen.

RELATIONSHIPS

DO YOU KNOW YOUR PURPOSE

Have you ever felt pressure from family members to do something their way? Have your parents directed or expected you to take a direction in life that you are convinced is not your course? Do you get diverted from your schedule to join your friends' schedule on a weekend? Have you failed to achieve your target at work because you followed your colleague's way of thinking or action?

When Jesus was 12 years old, he and his parents travelled with many others to Jerusalem for the Passover Festival. After a day's journey towards home, his parents discovered that Jesus was missing. It must have been annoying and frustrating.

Luke 2:44-50 says, *"but supposing him to have been in the company, they went a day's journey, and sought him among their relatives and acquaintances...Now so it was after three days they found him in the temple, sitting in the midst of the teachers, both*

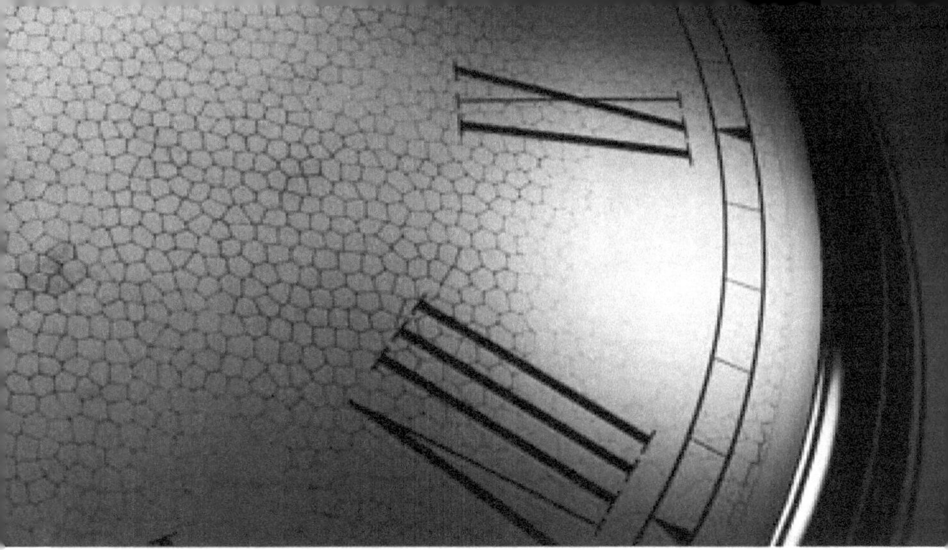

listening to them and asking them questions...and his mother said to him, 'Son, why have you done this to us? Look, your father and I have sought you anxiously."…. And he said to them, "Why did you seek me? Did you not know that I must be about my Father's business?" But they did not understand the statement which he spoke to them..." (NKJV)

Jesus knew why he had come and he was not going to let even his parents' programmes, schedules and engagements get in the way of fulfilling that purpose. His mind and mission were so clear (at least to him), that he had no shadow of doubt about who he needed to spend time with, where he needed to be, and even what conversations he needed to have. And that is why he could so confidently ask his earthly parents why they were looking for him because he needed to be in his father's house. In this, he was fulfilling his heavenly father's mandate for him here on earth.

DO YOU KNOW YOUR PURPOSE

Do you at times fail in your divine mandate and purpose because of trying too hard to make others understand and accept it? Not everyone will understand your mandate in life –your spouse, parents or children may not understand it. Your mandate is given to you from heaven and you have to be clear in your mind and spirit about your purpose. Don't work so hard to fit into other people's programmes or schedules if they do not align with your God-given purpose. Don't move with the crowd as you may be heading away from where you must be in order to fulfil your purpose. Jesus was missing in the group that was traveling back from Jerusalem, he was missing among the relatives, he was missing among the acquaintances, and he was not with the crowd. He stayed back **ALONE**! Alone sitting with the teachers in the temple – in his Father's house.

Dear child of God, know your mandate, discover your purpose, seek to understand where and with whom you must be, and then go confidently to fulfil your God-given purpose.

REFLECTIVE QUESTIONS

1. *Do you know and understand your purpose?*
2. *Are you working towards fulfilling that purpose?*
3. *How can you best align your attitudes, choices and actions with Christ's purpose for your life?*

. . . .

Lord, help me to know, understand and fulfil your purpose for my life and help me to align my life with it. Amen.

. . . .

STRUGGLING WITH A WAYWARD CHILD?

When you make that very personal decision and commitment to accept and follow the Lord Jesus Christ as your personal Saviour, it's a milestone decision. Then come the many promises in the Bible about all life is and has for you as a believer. But the way ahead is never promised to be smooth since on this earth, life is full of highs and lows, mountains and valleys, sunny and rainy days. Jesus himself promised that we would have trouble while we are in this world but at the same time encouraged us to find peace in him (John 16:33).

Our children are precious gifts and blessings in our lives and perhaps the result of much prayer. We want them to be nothing less than God-fearing and knowing him as their Lord. We want them to know the Lord as we do. But what if they don't? Things don't always work out the way we'd like them to. 1 Samuel 8:3 says, *"But his sons did not walk in his ways; they turned aside after dishonest gain, took bribes, and perverted justice."* In spite of Samuel's righteous and godly behaviour his son's did not follow his lead. Samuel had been dedicated to God since childhood. How could the children of such a righteous and devoted man be so ungodly, so corrupted and so perverted?

They caused Samuel a lot of pain. But it seems he still had some hope for them as he appointed them judges after his term. He was waiting for faith to manifest itself in them. But as far as we know it did not happen. At least the Bible does not give an account of their transformation journey. Nevertheless, Samuel kept his faith in God.

Are you that devoted Christian, diligently serving the Lord while at home your child gives you headaches? Take courage, your child's wayward and defiant behaviour does not impute guilt on you. Your son or daughter's walk in sinfulness must not come in the way of your faithfulness and service to the Almighty. Even when that child does not follow your godly ways, keep the faith and keep your eye on the prize. Let that not distract your focus. You have already planted the seed of faith in your child and the Lord himself grows and nurtures it.

STRUGGLING WITH A WAYWARD CHILD?

Remember your knowledge of the Lord as your Saviour and guide is absolutely personal and cannot be transferred directly to your child no matter how much you love them. They have their personal choice and decision to make, which is their responsibility not yours.

In 2 Kings 14:6 and Ezekiel 18, the Lord imputed on each person guilt for their own sin. No son shall bear the consequence of the father's sin and no father shall bear the consequence of a son's sin. As a parent, train up your child in righteousness and leave the rest to God (Proverbs 22:6).

1   *Do you value your children as gifts from God?*

2   *How are you stewarding their understanding of who God is?*

3   *How can you pray earnestly for them to walk with the Lord and experience His saving grace?*

. . . .

Lord, I thank you for the gift of children. Thank you that you found me fit to be the steward in bringing up my children. I am grateful for the chance to reflect you and your love to them. But Lord I also acknowledge that they have a very personal responsibility to make that life changing decision and choice to follow you and to walk in your ways. Draw them to yourself, dear Lord, that they too may experience your saving grace and enjoy eternity with you. Amen.

. . . .

WHAT A DEEP LOVE

What kind of love was this between David and Jonathan? How deep can love be between two friends who are neither spouses nor siblings? In 1 Samuel 20:4, Jonathan tells David, *"...whatever you want me to do, I'll do for you..."* This was in spite of what Jonathan's father, King Saul, wanted. This love was so deep that it transcended the father/son commitment.

1 Samuel 18:1-4 tell us that, *"After David had finished talking with Saul, Jonathan became one in spirit with David, and he loved him as himself... Jonathan took off the robe he was wearing and gave it to David, along with his tunic, and even his sword, his bow and his belt."* (NIV)

In life, we may have some connections like these but we must be very alert and sensitive to God's leading and direction to be able to derive value from them, which may seem irrational and impractical by any human standard. Those connections are God-made.

We can draw a comparison of such deep love with the love of Jesus Christ as he commands us in John 15:12-17 to love each other as he has loved us. He adds that, *"Greater love has no man than this: to lay down one's life for one's friends"* and we are his *"friends if you do what he commands."* He no longer calls us servants *"...because a servant does not know his master's business. Instead I have called you friends, for everything that I learned from my Father I have made known to you..."*

Jonathan was ready to leak his father Saul's secrets and agenda to David to save his treasured friend David's life. Jesus has equally made known to us everything that he learned from his Father and for that reason we are no longer servants but friends and heirs with him. Just as Jonathan readily handed over his robe, tunic and sword to David (which sounds like handing over or sharing his sonship and his inheritance with David), so has Jesus lovingly shared and invited us to partake in the inheritance of his Father's Kingdom by so willingly coming

down to this earth, becoming a man and laying down his life for us. What a divine love! What a privilege. Must we not love Him back with our everything? Should we not value that grace? We did not deserve it but freely and lovingly He gave it.

REFLECTIVE QUESTIONS

1   *Do you have a friendship of genuine and unconditional love?*

2   *How does your relationship with that special friend reflect your relationship with Christ?*

Dear Lord, through the demonstration of genuine and unconditional love from a friend, I pray that you help me not only acknowledge, but also appreciate your priceless gift of love to me. Being God, you gave your life as ransom to reconcile me to the Father. May I never forget your sacrifice and may I every day love you and those you have put into my life. Amen.

My Reflections

MY MOTHER AND MY BROTHERS

Naturally speaking, it is a great abomination to disown one's relative and especially a parent and siblings. One would be considered mad or unfeeling to disown their parents or siblings, let alone voice it out loud in the presence of many witnesses. Yet this is exactly what Jesus did.

This scripture clearly teaches us that once we accept the Lord Jesus Christ as our Saviour and begin to do God's will, we become family. That is, those who believe and are transformed become one family under God. This does not in any way abolish the biological families that we belong to. Yet internal connections link us with others in the faith who have acquired sonship through faith in Jesus Christ. We have become co-heirs with them in Christ.

This connection also makes us ambassadors for Christ as Paul puts it in 2 Corinthians 5:20, as though God were making his appeal through us.

Let us therefore jealously guard the relationships that we acquire through salvation as well as reaching out to our earthly mothers, fathers, brothers and sisters so that they may equally become our spiritual relatives by accepting the Lord as their Saviour and doing God's will. We must implore them and pray for them to be reconciled to God. How are we carrying it out practically? We shall be held to account when the time comes and so we must diligently work for the Lord so that we are found to be faithful at the end.

REFLECTIVE QUESTIONS

1   *Do you have a spiritual family with whom you enjoy a family relationship?*

2   *How jealously do you guard that spiritual family relationship?*

3   *How do you reach out to your earthly family to appeal to them to be reconciled to God and become part of your spiritual family?*

. . . .

Lord, help me play my role in my spiritual family as you have purposed for my life. Amen.

. . . .

CHOSEN, ROYAL AND HOLY

When it's competition time, the players are keen on being chosen to represent their teams and in international sport, to represent their country and hopefully win the game to proudly fly their country's flag for the world to see.

In kingdoms, the royal family may be the envy of many because they enjoy so many privileges just for being royal and having been born into that family. They didn't work for it. They didn't compete for it. They didn't even apply for it. They are just born into royalty.

If you are chosen as an athlete to represent your team or country or if you are royalty, whether inside your kingdom or while visiting some other place, you must espouse and reflect the values and standards of the team, the country or the kingdom that you represent. You must play by the rules of those who sent you.

So is it for us who have now been called out of darkness into this wonderful light. We have thus received an adoption into sonship and we are now a chosen people. God chose us before creation (Ephesians 1:4) and we are a kind of first fruit of all his creation (James 1:18). We are a royal priesthood having been born into the family of God in the spirit – not by anything we have ourselves done, we did not deserve it, but we are born into it through God's mercy and so we have become a heavenly royalty.

Having been chosen of God and born by the spirit into his family, we have to represent and reflect a holy God (Leviticus 11:45; 1 Peter 1:16). And having been bought at a price (1 Corinthians 6:19-20), we have now become God's possession because he indeed paid a special price for us (John 3:16). If you go into a store and buy something and pay full price for it, you proudly own it and it becomes your treasured possession. In fact, the more you pay for an item, the more preciously treasured it will be. That is the kind of possession we are to the Father who, out of his abundance of love for us, paid the greatest price one could ever pay for our ransom.

Therefore, having been chosen by God himself, and born into his family in the spirit (John 1:13; 3:5, 8) we are blessed to partake of the inheritance in the kingdom with the Son who gave his life that we may become heirs with him (Romans 8:17).

REFLECTIVE QUESTIONS

1   *Are you aware of your genetic line in the spiritual realm?*

2   *Do you know you are a royal breed?*

3   *How can you represent your 'royal family' relationship in your everyday life?*

Dear Lord, help me recognize my genetic line in your family and kingdom. As a chosen representative of your divine royalty, help me to competently and diligently live out your personality as I reflect your holiness in my everyday life. Amen.

My Reflections

www.ingramcontent.com/pod-product-compliance
Lightning Source LLC
Chambersburg PA
CBHW031738150726
47989CB00006B/2512